Caterpillar to Butterfly

by Lisa M. Herrington

Content Consultant

Elizabeth Case DeSantis, M.A. Elementary Education
Julia A. Stark Elementary School, Stamford, Connecticut

Reading Consultant

Jeanne M. Clidas, Ph.D.
Reading Specialist

Children's Press®
An Imprint of Scholastic Inc.
New York Toronto London Auckland Sydney
Mexico City New Delhi Hong Kong
Danbury, Connecticut

Library of Congress Cataloging-in-Publication Data
Herrington, Lisa M.
  Caterpillar to butterfly/by Lisa M. Herrington; content consultant Elizabeth Case
DeSantis, M.A. Elementary Education, Grade 2 Teacher, Julia A. Stark Elementary,
Stamford, Connecticut; reading consultant, Jeanne Clidas, Ph.D.
      pages cm. — (Rookie read-about science)
  Includes index.
  Audience: Age 3 - 6.
  ISBN 978-0-531-21055-0 (library binding) — ISBN 978-0-531-24976-5 (pbk.)
  1. Butterflies—Life cycles—Juvenile literature. 2. Butterflies—Metamorphosis—
Juvenile literature. 3. Caterpillars--Juvenile literature. I. Title.

  QL544.2.H464 2014
  595.78'9—dc23   2013034813

Produced by Spooky Cheetah Press
Design by Keith Plechaty

© 2014 by Scholastic Inc.

Printed in China 62

SCHOLASTIC, CHILDREN'S PRESS, ROOKIE READ-ABOUT®, and associated logos are
trademarks and/or registered trademarks of Scholastic Inc.

1 2 3 4 5 6 7 8 9 10 R 23 22 21 20 19 18 17 16 15 14

Photographs © 2014: Dreamstime/eronika Trofer: 30; Getty Images: 4
(johnnylemonseed), cover top left, 7, 26 top, 31 bottom (ParkerDeen); iStockphoto/
CathyKeifer: 12; Media Bakery: 29 (James Urbach), cover top right, 15, 27 bottom, 31
center bottom; Science Source: 28 bottom (Gary Meszaros), 24, 31 top (Steve & Dave
Maslowski), 23 (Thomas & Pat Leeson); Shutterstock, Inc.: 8, 27 top (Cathy Keifer),
20, 26 bottom (Goran Kapor), cover bottom (Lightspring); Superstock, Inc.: 28 top
(Biosphoto), 16 (Lee Canfield); The Image Works/The Natural History Museum: cover
top center, 11, 31 center top; Thinkstock: 3 top right (Hemera), 3 top left, 3 bottom, 19
(iStockphoto).

Table of Contents

Monarch Butterfly

wings

head

thorax

abdomen

wings

antennae

legs

Winged Beauties

A **butterfly** is an insect. It has four wings, six legs, and two antennae. It also has three body parts: head, thorax, and abdomen.

There are about 17,000 kinds of butterflies in the world.

5

From Egg to Caterpillar

A monarch is one kind of butterfly. All butterflies change as they grow. The change is called metamorphosis (met-uh-MOR-fuh-siss). It is the butterfly's life cycle. A butterfly's life cycle begins with an **egg**.

Some female butterflies, such as monarchs, lay eggs one at a time. Others lay them in groups.

egg

This photo shows the steps it takes for a caterpillar to break out of its egg.

The egg hatches a few days after it is laid. A tiny **caterpillar** bites through the egg. Then it crawls out.

FUN FACT!

A caterpillar's first meal is its eggshell!

The caterpillar is very hungry. It eats leaves to grow. It starts with the leaf it was born on.

Caterpillars eat a lot of leaves! They grow fast.

This is a combination of three photos. It shows how a caterpillar sheds its skin.

As the caterpillar gets bigger, its skin becomes snug. It sheds its skin four or five times. This is called molting.

FUN FACT!

Monarch caterpillars and butterflies are poisonous. Their bright colors warn animals not to eat them.

From Caterpillar to Chrysalis

After two weeks, the caterpillar is fully grown. It finds a place to rest. It forms a hard shell called a **chrysalis** (KRISS-uh-liss).

FUN FACT!

A caterpillar hangs upside down to make a chrysalis.

chrysalis

The caterpillar stays in the chrysalis for about two weeks. A big change takes place inside. The caterpillar is turning into a butterfly.

The chrysalis is clear right before the butterfly comes out.

Fly, Butterfly!

The chrysalis breaks open. A beautiful adult butterfly pushes out.

FUN FACT!

Most butterflies live for a few weeks. Some monarchs live up to nine months.

The butterfly is now in the final part of its life cycle.

Within a few hours, the butterfly's wings will harden. Then it can fly.

The butterfly's wings are wet and wrinkled. It cannot fly yet. The butterfly stays where it hatched until its wings dry.

FUN FACT!

A butterfly's wings are covered with thin scales.

The monarch flies away. It spends much of its life feeding on flowers. A butterfly has no teeth. It uses a special tube on its head to drink nectar. A flower's liquid nectar gives the butterfly energy to fly.

A butterfly's tube works like a straw. It curls up when not in use.

A mother butterfly finds a milkweed plant. She lays her eggs. The life cycle begins again.

FUN FACT!

It takes about a month for an egg to become a butterfly.

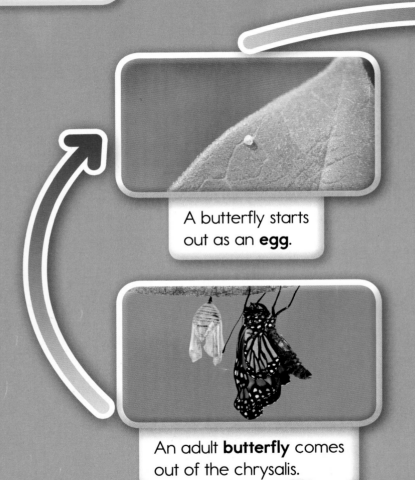

A butterfly starts out as an **egg**.

An adult **butterfly** comes out of the chrysalis.

Life Cycle

Think About It

What is the first step in a butterfly's life?

Where does a caterpillar change into a butterfly?

When is the butterfly ready to fly?

A **caterpillar** hatches from the egg.

The caterpillar forms a shell called a **chrysalis**.

27

Butterflies live on every continent except Antarctica. They start as eggs that grow into caterpillars.

The female Queen Alexandra's birdwing is the world's largest butterfly. It is about the length of a football from wing to wing. This butterfly lives in Papua New Guinea.

A black swallowtail butterfly's back wings look like they have tails. There are more than 500 types of swallowtails in the world.

Butterflies

Buckeyes have giant spots on their wings that look like eyes. The spots scare off birds and insects. These butterflies can be found in the United States.

Let's Explore!

Look for butterflies outside or ask an adult to help you find photos of them online or in a book. Keep a journal and make drawings of the butterflies you see. Include your observations: What are the butterfly's colors, patterns, and wing shape? Where did you spot it? What was it doing?

Food Chain

Living things depend on each other to survive. Butterflies get their food from flowers. Butterflies also become food for birds, mice, insects, and other creatures. These creatures need food as they move through their own life cycles. This is called a food chain.

Flower

A flower blooms.

Butterfly

A monarch butterfly feeds off the flower.

Bird

Certain kinds of birds eat the monarch. They are not affected by the monarch's poison.

Glossary

butterfly (BUHT-ur-fly): a winged insect with three body parts, six legs, and two antennae

caterpillar (KAT-ur-pil-ur): a long, wormlike creature that changes into a butterfly

chrysalis (KRISS-uh-liss): the hard shell in which the caterpillar turns into a butterfly

egg (eg): the place where the caterpillar grows

Index

Facts for Now

Visit this Scholastic Web site for more information on butterflies:
www.factsfornow.scholastic.com
Enter the keyword **Butterflies**

About the Author

Lisa M. Herrington writes books and articles for kids. She lives in Trumbull, Connecticut, with her husband, Ryan, and daughter, Caroline. They have several flowering bushes around their home that attract beautiful butterflies.

32